Visit
NORTHERN
IRELAND

NORTHERN
IRELAND

EUROPE

ASIA

NORTH
AMERICA

AFRICA

SOUTH
AMERICA

AUSTRALIA

Chris Oxlade and Anita Ganeri

www.heinemann.co.uk/library

Visit our website to find out more information about **Heinemann Library** books.

To order:
☎ Phone 44 (0) 1865 888066
📄 Send a fax to 44 (0) 1865 314091
💻 Visit the Heinemann Bookshop at www.heinemann.co.uk/library to browse our catalogue and order online.

First published in Great Britain by Heinemann Library, Halley Court, Jordan Hill, Oxford OX2 8EJ, part of Harcourt Education. Heinemann is a registered trademark of Harcourt Education Ltd.

Editorial: Nicole Irving and Georga Godwin
Design: Ron Kamen and StoreyBooks
Picture Research: Catherine Bevan and Ginny Stroud-Lewis
Production: Sévy Ribierre

Originated by Dot Gradations Ltd
Printed and bound in China by South China Printing Company

ISBN 0 431 08273 1 (hardback)
07 06 05 04 03
10 9 8 7 6 5 4 3 2 1

ISBN 0 431 08278 2 (paperback)
08 07 06 05 04
10 9 8 7 6 5 4 3 2 1

British Library Cataloguing in Publication Data

Oxlade, Chris and Ganeri, Anita
Visit Northern Ireland
914.1'6
A full catalogue record for this book is available from the British Library.

Acknowledgements

The Publishers would like to thank the following for permission to reproduce photographs: Belfast Telegraph pp. **20, 23**; Collections/Geray Sweeney p. **26**; Collections/Image Ireland/Alain Le Garsmeur p. **24**; Collections/Image Ireland/John Lennon p. **27**; Collections/Image Ireland/Geray Sweeney p. **22**; Corbis pp. **15, 29**; Dewynters p. **28**; PA Photos p. **14**; Peter Evans pp. **5, 6, 7, 8, 9, 10, 11, 12, 13, 16, 17, 18, 19, 21**; Robert Harding/C. Bowman p. **25**.

Cover photograph of the Giant's Causeway, reproduced with permission of Corbis\ Ric Ergenbright.

Every effort has been made to contact copyright holders of any material reproduced in this book. Any omissions will be rectified in subsequent printings if notice is given to the Publishers.

Contents

Any words appearing in bold, **like this**, are explained in the Glossary.

Northern Ireland

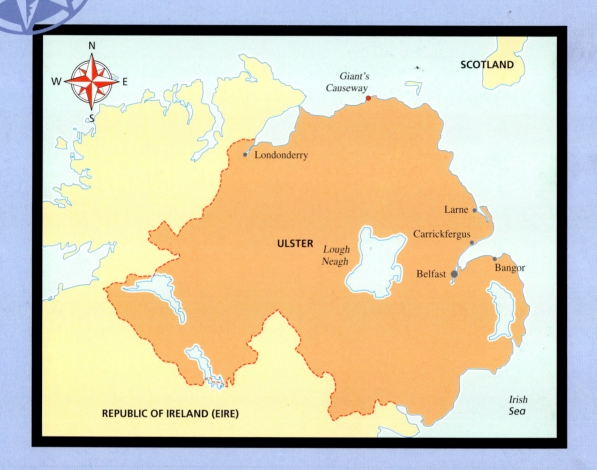

Northern Ireland is a country in the United Kingdom. It is part of an island called Ireland. About one and a half million people live in Northern Ireland.

4

The **capital** city of Northern Ireland is called Belfast. The city is built around the River Lagan, which leads to the Irish Sea. Can you spot the **shipyards**?

Land

There are lots of gentle, grassy hills in Northern Ireland. There are some mountains, too. The **coast** is very beautiful, with steep cliffs and sheltered bays.

In the centre of Northern Ireland is a
huge lake called Lough Neagh. It is
20 kilometres (12 miles) wide. It is the
largest lake in the United Kingdom.

Landmarks

This castle is called Carrickfergus Castle. It stands next to Carrickfergus **harbour**. People started building it more than 800 years ago. It is Northern Ireland's most famous castle.

This is the Giant's Causeway, on the north coast. A causeway is a path across wet or muddy land. Stories say a giant called Finn MacCool built it.

Homes

About half the people of Northern Ireland live in Belfast or in towns nearby. Many of them live in **terraced** houses or blocks of flats like these.

In the countryside, some people still live in small, **thatched** cottages. Most people now live in modern **bungalows** or houses like this one, which are sometimes brightly painted.

Food

Most Irish food is simply flavoured. Irish stew is very popular. It is made from meat and vegetables, and is nearly always served with potatoes.

Bakers in Northern Ireland make a **traditional** bread from flour, soda and buttermilk. It is called soda bread. It is delicious hot, straight from the oven.

Clothes

Young people in Northern Ireland normally wear casual clothes. Sometimes they dress up in **national costume**. These girls are wearing their **traditional** dresses.

Some children wear **uniforms** for school. At some schools pupils wear shirts and ties. At others, pupils wear school sweatshirts.

Work

Many people in Northern Ireland work in engineering companies, making all sorts of machines. Workers build and repair huge ships in Belfast's **shipyards**.

Many people work as farmers. They grow **crops** and raise animals, such as cattle and sheep. Here farmers are buying and selling cattle at a weekly market.

Transcript

Large ships called **ferries** carry people, cars, buses and lorries between Northern Ireland and the other countries of the United Kingdom. Northern Ireland's biggest **port** is called Larne.

A railway runs between the cities of Belfast and Londonderry. Trains also go to Eire (Republic of Ireland), which makes up the rest of the island of Ireland.

Language

Most people in Northern Ireland speak English. They often speak English with a Northern Irish accent. This can be tricky for other English speakers to understand at first.

Most newspapers and magazines are written in English. There are **national** newspapers for the whole of Northern Ireland and **local** newspapers, like this one.

School

Children in Northern Ireland go to Christian schools, which are either Catholic or Protestant. A few schools are open to everyone.

In the countryside, children go to small **primary** schools. There may not be many children in each class. Many children travel to school by bus.

Free time

This photograph shows Gaelic football, a popular game in Northern Ireland. The rules of the game are a mixture of soccer and rugby rules.

On weekends and during school holidays, children in Northern Ireland enjoy going to the seaside. Bangor is the largest seaside **resort**. It is on the east **coast**.

Celebrations

St Patrick is the **patron saint** of the Republic and Northern Ireland.
St Patrick's Day is 17 March. Many towns and villages hold colourful parades to remember his life.

The Royal Ulster Show is an important event for Northern Ireland's farmers. Each year, they bring their best cattle and other animals to the show to display them.

The Arts

Arts **festivals** are held all over Northern Ireland, displaying different sorts of art. The most important one takes place in Belfast, in November.

A ceilidh is a **traditional** Irish band. People play instruments such as drums, violins and pipes in a ceilidh. Their music is lively and perfect for dancing.

Factfile

Name	Northern Ireland is part of the United Kingdom of Great Britain and Northern Ireland.
Capital	The capital city is Belfast.
Languages	English is the official language of Northern Ireland. Some people also speak a language called Irish Gaelic.
Population	About one and a half million people live here.
Money	In England and all the other countries in the United Kingdom the money is called pounds sterling (£). There are 100 pence in the pound.
Religion	Most people in Northern Ireland are Christians. About two-thirds are Protestants and one third are Catholics.
Products	Northern Ireland produces machinery, ships and boats, aircraft, textiles and livestock.

Irish Gaelic words you can learn

aon (say: ayn)	one
dó (say: doe)	two
tri (say: three)	three
tá (say: thaw)	yes
níl (say: knee)	no
dia dhuit (say: dee-a-gwit)	hello
slán agat (say: slawn-aguth)	goodbye
le do thoil (say: le-do-hull)	please

Glossary

accent	way words sound when people say them
bungalow	house with only one main floor
capital	most important city in a country
coast	edge of the land where it meets the sea
crops	vegetables grown for food
ferry	ship that carries people, cars and trucks across water from one place to another
festival	celebration, where lots of different events take place
harbour	sheltered place that boats go in and out of
local	things that are near by
national	to do with a whole country
national costume	clothes that people used to wear in the past in a particular country
official	set up by the people who run the country
patron saint	saint who is said to look after a country
port	place where ships tie up before going to sea
primary school	for children between 5 and 11 years old
resort	place that has a lot for visitors to do
shipyards	place where ships are built
terraced	houses that are joined together in a row
thatched	houses that have a roof made of straw
traditional	something that has been done the same way for many years
uniform	clothes that people wear to all look the same

Index

The British Union is the **official** flag of Northern Ireland, but many people who live there would like to change it.